Putting Your Affairs In Order
&
Getting The Last Word

Whether you're in the prime of your life or the Autumn of your life it's a good idea to plan for the unfortunate event of not being able to manage your own affairs.

Completing the information set out in this book will not only help to put your affairs in order, it will help your family and friends to manage them if need be.

Then when your time comes as it must to all of us, it will be so much easier for friends and loved ones to make sure your wishes are carried out. Pardon the pun but you can truly rest in peace.

So what are you waiting for, make sure you're organised and get the last word in.

Sections

- Personal Details

- Personal Details (Health & Medical)

- Finance Details

- Immediate Family Contact Details

- Other Family & Friends

- House Keeping Information

- Insurance Policy Information

- My Digital Presence

- Keep It To Yourself

- Collection Of Important Documents

- Getting The Last Word

Forward Notes

Please note that it is important to keep this book in a secure and safe place known only to yourself and a trusted friend, family member or professional such as a solicitor.

Everyone's situation is different so whilst we have included lots of detail we have also included some completely blank templates in case you wish to add more detail.

The information contained in here is not bound by law and therefore it is wise to ensure that your will is made and kept up to date.

Once the book is complete make a note for yourself to check through the information again, at least once a year making any necessary changes needed.

Personal Details

First Name/s	
Surname	
Maiden Name	
Status	Single □ Married □ Widowed □ Divorced □ Other □
Previous Names	
Present Address/ Phone Number	
Status	Employed □ Self Employed □ Unemployed □ Retired □ Other □
Occupation	
Employers/ Business Name & Contact Details	
Date Of Birth	
Place Of Birth	
NI Number	
UTR (Tex Ref)	
Passport Number	
Religion	
Spouse/Partner & Contact Details	
Next Of Kin & Contact Details	
Spare Key Holders Contact Details	

Personal Details

Health & Medical Information

Doctors Name	
Surgery Contact Numbers	
Blood Group	
Allergies	
Any Controlled Conditions For Example High Blood Pressure	
Details of Any Regular Medication Requirements Prescribed Or Otherwise	

Personal Details

Health & Medical Information

Details Of Any Surgical Operations	
Details Of Any Physical Disabilities	
Details Of Any Mental Disabilities	
Details of Special Dietary Needs	

Personal Details

Health & Medical Information

If I am severely and permanently mentally impaired, here are my wishes

Life Support Machine?

YES ☐ Keep me alive as long as you can no matter what the chances are

NO ☐ No I don't want to be kept alive by a machine

Other/reasons:

CPR?

YES ☐ Make my heart start beating again if possible no matter what

NO ☐ I don't what to come back it was meant to be so leave me

Other/reasons:

Personal Details

Health & Medical Information

Any Other Medical Issues You Need To Mention

Finance Details

Bank & Building Society Accounts

Bank/BSoc. Name	A/C Number	Sort Code	Type Of A/C

Other Finances Stocks Shares, Bonds etc.

Name Of Company	Details

Finance Details

Debit & Credit Cards

Company/Bank	Card Numbers	Type Of Card

Store Accounts For Example Clothing Catalogue

Name Of Company	Details

Finance Details

Mortgages & Loans

Bank/Loan Co.	Reference - A/C Number	Mortgage/Loan
Property Address If Mortgage Or Other Details If Not		
Bank/Loan Co.	Reference - A/C Number	Mortgage/Loan
Property Address If Mortgage Or Other Details If Not		
Bank/Loan Co.	Reference - A/C Number	Mortgage/Loan
Property Address If Mortgage Or Other Details If Not		
Bank/Loan Co.	Reference - A/C Number	Mortgage/Loan
Property Address If Mortgage Or Other Details If Not		
Bank/Loan Co.	Reference - A/C Number	Mortgage/Loan
Property Address If Mortgage Or Other Details If Not		

Other Notes On Property/Loans

Finance Details

Mortgages & Loans

Bank/Loan Co.	Reference - A/C Number	Mortgage/Loan
Property Address If Mortgage Or Other Details If Not		
Bank/Loan Co.	Reference - A/C Number	Mortgage/Loan
Property Address If Mortgage Or Other Details If Not		
Bank/Loan Co.	Reference - A/C Number	Mortgage/Loan
Property Address If Mortgage Or Other Details If Not		
Bank/Loan Co.	Reference - A/C Number	Mortgage/Loan
Property Address If Mortgage Or Other Details If Not		
Bank/Loan Co.	Reference - A/C Number	Mortgage/Loan
Property Address If Mortgage Or Other Details If Not		

Other Notes On Property/Loans

Finance Details

Property Owned/Part Owned

Details Of Ownership/Rental Details If Applicable

Property Address

Details Of Ownership/Rental Details If Applicable

Property Address

Details Of Ownership/Rental Details If Applicable

Property Address

Other Information for Example - Letting Agent Contact Details

Finance Details

Property Owned/Part Owned

Details Of Ownership/Rental Details If Applicable

Property Address

Details Of Ownership/Rental Details If Applicable

Property Address

Details Of Ownership/Rental Details If Applicable

Property Address

Other Information for Example - Letting Agent Contact Details

Finance Details

Property Owned/Part Owned

Details Of Ownership/Rental Details If Applicable

Property Address

Details Of Ownership/Rental Details If Applicable

Property Address

Details Of Ownership/Rental Details If Applicable

Property Address

Other Information for Example - Letting Agent Contact Details

Finance Details

Direct Debits & Standing Orders In Force

DD/SO	Payable to	Date Paid Out	Frequency	Bank Name

Finance Details

Direct Debits & Standing Orders In Force

DD/SO	Payable to	Date Paid Out	Frequency	Bank Name

Finance Details

Direct Debits & Standing Orders In Force

DD/SO	Payable to	Date Paid Out	Frequency	Bank Name

Finance Details

Payments Committed To **NOT PAID Via DD/SO**

Payment For	Due Date	Frequency	Payable To

Finance Details

Payments Committed To **NOT PAID Via DD/SO**

Payment For	Due Date	Frequency	Payable To

Finance Details

Incoming Monies Pensions/Earnings/Benefits Etc.

Source Of Income

Reference

Contact

Other Info.

Source Of Income

Reference

Contact

Other Info.

Source Of Income

Reference

Contact

Other Info.

Source Of Income

Reference

Contact

Other Info.

Finance Details

Incoming Monies Pensions/Earnings/Benefits Etc.

Source Of Income

Reference

Contact

Other Info.

Source Of Income

Reference

Contact

Other Info.

Source Of Income

Reference

Contact

Other Info.

Source Of Income

Reference

Contact

Other Info.

Finance Details

Annuity Pension Schemes etc.

Details Of Any Schemes/Plans Not Yet Taken Up Including Death In Service
And Any Funeral Provisions Already Made

Company	Reference
Contact	
Other Info.	

Company	Reference
Contact	
Other Info.	

Company	Reference
Contact	
Other Info.	

Company	Reference
Contact	
Other Info.	

Finance Details

Annuity Pension Schemes etc.

Details Of Any Schemes/Plans Not Yet Taken Up Including Death In Service
And Any Funeral Provisions Already Made

Company	Reference
Contact	
Other Info.	

Company	Reference
Contact	
Other Info.	

Company	Reference
Contact	
Other Info.	

Company	Reference
Contact	
Other Info.	

Immediate Family Contact Details

Name   Relationship

Address

_____

_____

Telephone

Name   Relationship

Address

_____

_____

Telephone

Name   Relationship

Address

_____

_____

Telephone

Name   Relationship

Address

_____

_____

Telephone

Name   Relationship

Address

_____

_____

Telephone

Immediate Family Contact Details

Name   Relationship

Address

Telephone

Name   Relationship

Address

Telephone

Name   Relationship

Address

Telephone

Name   Relationship

Address

Telephone

Name   Relationship

Address

Telephone

Immediate Family Contact Details

Name   Relationship

Address

Telephone

Name   Relationship

Address

Telephone

Name   Relationship

Address

Telephone

Name   Relationship

Address

Telephone

Name   Relationship

Address

Telephone

Immediate Family Contact Details

Name   Relationship

Address

Telephone

Name   Relationship

Address

Telephone

Name   Relationship

Address

Telephone

Name   Relationship

Address

Telephone

Name   Relationship

Address

Telephone

Immediate Family Contact Details

Name   Relationship

Address

Telephone

Name   Relationship

Address

Telephone

Name   Relationship

Address

Telephone

Name   Relationship

Address

Telephone

Name   Relationship

Address

Telephone

Immediate Family Contact Details

Name	Relationship

Address

Telephone

Name	Relationship

Address

Telephone

Name	Relationship

Address

Telephone

Name	Relationship

Address

Telephone

Name	Relationship

Address

Telephone

Other Family & Friends

Name	Contact Details

Other Family & Friends

Name	Contact Details

Other Family & Friends

Name	Contact Details

Other Family & Friends

Name	Contact Details

House Keeping Information

	Utility Provider Details
Gas	Contact:-
Account Number	
Other Info.	
Electricity	Contact:-
Account Number	
Other Info.	
Water	Contact:-
Account Number	
Other Info.	
Land-line Phone	Contact:-
Account Number	
Other Info.	
Mobile Phone	Contact:-
Account Number	
Other Info.	
Security Alarms	Contact:-
Account Number	
Other Info.	
Internet	Contact:-
Account Number	
Other Info.	
Satellite TV	Contact:-
Account Number	
Other Info.	
	Contact:-
Account Number	
Other Info.	

House Keeping Information

Utility Provider Details

	Contact:-
Account Number	
Other Info.	
	Contact:-
Account Number	
Other Info.	
	Contact:-
Account Number	
Other Info.	
	Contact:-
Account Number	
Other Info.	
	Contact:-
Account Number	
Other Info.	
	Contact:-
Account Number	
Other Info.	
	Contact:-
Account Number	
Other Info.	
	Contact:-
Account Number	
Other Info.	
	Contact:-
Account Number	
Other Info.	

House Keeping Information

Service Provider Details	
Electrician	Contact:-
Other Info.	
Plumber	Contact:-
Other Info.	
Handy Man	Contact:-
Other Info.	
Gardener	Contact:-
Other Info.	
Window Cleaner	Contact:-
Other Info.	
Gas Engineer	Contact:-
Other Info.	
Locksmith	Contact:-
Other Info.	
Cleaner	Contact:-
Other Info.	
Laundry	Contact:-
Other Info.	

House Keeping Information

Service Provider Details	
Solicitor	Contact:-
Other Info.	
Accountant	Contact:-
Other Info.	
Financial Adviser	Contact:-
Other Info.	
	Contact:-
Other Info.	
	Contact:-
Other Info.	
	Contact:-
Other Info.	
	Contact:-
Other Info.	
	Contact:-
Other Info.	
	Contact:-
Other Info.	

Insurance Policy Information

Cover For **Home Contents**	Company Name & Contact Details:
Policy Number	

Cover For **Home Buildings**	Company Name & Contact Details:
Policy Number	

Cover For **Travel**	Company Name & Contact Details:
Policy Number	

Cover For **Life**	Company Name & Contact Details:
Policy Number	

Cover For **Medical**	Company Name & Contact Details:
Policy Number	

Cover For **Dental**	Company Name & Contact Details:
Policy Number	

Insurance Policy Information

Cover For	Company Name & Contact Details:
Car Registration-	
Policy Number	

Cover For	Company Name & Contact Details:
Car Registration-	
Policy Number	

Cover For	Company Name & Contact Details:
Policy Number	

Cover For	Company Name & Contact Details:
Policy Number	

Cover For	Company Name & Contact Details:
Policy Number	

Cover For	Company Name & Contact Details:
Policy Number	

Insurance Policy Information

Cover For	Company Name & Contact Details:
Policy Number	

Cover For	Company Name & Contact Details:
Policy Number	

Cover For	Company Name & Contact Details:
Policy Number	

Cover For	Company Name & Contact Details:
Policy Number	

Cover For	Company Name & Contact Details:
Policy Number	

Cover For	Company Name & Contact Details:
Policy Number	

My Digital Presence

Social Media Email Accounts Etc.

On-Line Account	Usernames/Passwords Login Details
Facebook	
Twitter	

My Digital Presence

Social Media Email Accounts Etc.

On-Line Account	Usernames/Passwords Login Details

Keep It To Yourself

Off Line Passwords, Key Codes, Pin Numbers

Pin/Code Number	For Use With	Other Info.

Keep It To Yourself

Off Line Passwords, Key Codes, Pin Numbers

Pin/Code Number	For Use With	Other Info.

Collection Of Important Documents

Can Be Found Here:	

Check List	
Document	✓
Birth Certificate	
Name Change/Adoption Papers (if applicable)	
Marriage Certificate	
Divorce Papers (if applicable)	
Passport	
Driving Licence	
Car Registration Docs.	
Car MOT Certificate	
Car Insurance Certificate	
Home Insurance Certificate	
Bank Statements & Pass Books	
Stocks Shares Docs.	
Annuity Docs.	
Pension Docs.	
Loan Agreements	
Mortgage Papers	
House Deeds	
Tax Forms/Papers	
Pay Slips	
Utility Bills	
Warranties & Receipts	
Power Of Attorney Docs.	
Donor Card	
Last Will & Testimony	
Living Will	

Collection Of Important Documents

Document	✓

Collection Of Important Documents

Document	✓

Collection Of Important Documents

Document	✓

Collection Of Important Documents

Document	✓

Collection Of Important Documents

Document	✓

Collection Of Important Documents

Document	✓

Getting The Last Word

My Preferred Funeral Arrangements

Burial or Cremation ?

If Cremation What To Do With Ashes

If Burial Where To Be Buried & Special Epitaph Requirements

Religious Service In Place Of Worship,Crematorium Or Other?

If Place Of Worship Where Would You Like

If Other Explain

Getting The Last Word

My Preferred Funeral Arrangements

Flowers & Wreaths, Just Family Anyone Or None

Dress Code For Funeral Smart Black Or Other?

Your Outfit Preference

Any Preference For Type Of Coffin

Donations; If So For What Cause?

Your Favourite Hymns/Prayers

Music You Want To Be Played

Getting The Last Word

My Preferred Funeral Arrangements

Words of Thanks And Special Mentions You Would Like Somebody To Read Out On Your Behalf.

Getting The Last Word

My Preferred Funeral Arrangements

Other Notes On Funeral Arrangements

Getting The Last Word

My Preferred Funeral Arrangements

Other Notes On Funeral Arrangements

Getting The Last Word

And Now The Party's Over

I Have Made A Will You Will Find Details With

Executors Of The Will Are

Getting The Last Word

Other Notes & Extra Information

Getting The Last Word

Other Notes & Extra Information

Getting The Last Word

Other Notes & Extra Information

Getting The Last Word

Other Notes & Extra Information

Getting The Last Word

Other Notes & Extra Information

Getting The Last Word

Other Notes & Extra Information

Getting The Last Word

Other Notes & Extra Information

Getting The Last Word

Other Notes & Extra Information

Getting The Last Word

Other Notes & Extra Information

Getting The Last Word

Other Notes & Extra Information

Getting The Last Word

Other Notes & Extra Information

Getting The Last Word

Other Notes & Extra Information

Getting The Last Word

Other Notes & Extra Information

Getting The Last Word

Other Notes & Extra Information

Getting The Last Word

Other Notes & Extra Information

Getting The Last Word

Other Notes & Extra Information

Getting The Last Word

Other Notes & Extra Information

Getting The Last Word

Other Notes & Extra Information

Getting The Last Word

Other Notes & Extra Information

Getting The Last Word

Other Notes & Extra Information

Getting The Last Word

Other Notes & Extra Information

Getting The Last Word

Other Notes & Extra Information

Getting The Last Word

Other Notes & Extra Information

Getting The Last Word

Other Notes & Extra Information

Getting The Last Word

Other Notes & Extra Information

Getting The Last Word

Other Notes & Extra Information

Getting The Last Word

Other Notes & Extra Information

Getting The Last Word

Other Notes & Extra Information

Getting The Last Word

Other Notes & Extra Information

Getting The Last Word

Other Notes & Extra Information

Getting The Last Word

Other Notes & Extra Information

Getting The Last Word

Other Notes & Extra Information

Getting The Last Word

Other Notes & Extra Information

Getting The Last Word

Other Notes & Extra Information

Getting The Last Word

Other Notes & Extra Information

Getting The Last Word

Other Notes & Extra Information

Getting The Last Word

Other Notes & Extra Information

Getting The Last Word

Other Notes & Extra Information

Getting The Last Word

Other Notes & Extra Information

Getting The Last Word

Other Notes & Extra Information

Getting The Last Word

Other Notes & Extra Information

Getting The Last Word

Other Notes & Extra Information

Getting The Last Word

Other Notes & Extra Information

Getting The Last Word

Other Notes & Extra Information

Getting The Last Word

Other Notes & Extra Information